JUGGLING

Written by Linda Stephenson

Illustrated by Phi

D1609618

HENDERSON
An imprint of DK Publishing, Inc.

HI!

Welcome to the wild world of juggling! Have you ever wanted to juggle, but didn't know how to go about doing it? Can you juggle a little bit already, but want to do more? Well, here's your chance.

Read on and enter the Juggling Zone, the world where the impossible can be made to happen. That is, you can learn to throw and catch three or more objects with only two hands. That does sound pretty impossible, doesn't it?

Well, it might, but juggling has been going on for centuries. Its origins are lost in the mist of time. We do know that someone has gone on record juggling at the court of the ancient Egyptian pharaohs. And good old Socrates said that he saw a woman juggling twelve hoops. Wow! The ancient Romans even had a word in their vocabulary for a juggler. (It's "ventilator.") Spooky, eh? And, someone told me that the old French word for "magician" was juggler. Huh?

STOP BUGGIN ME!

But I digress. The Juggling Zone awaits. So read on . . . .

JUGGLING
FOR COWARDS

We'll begin at the beginning, with those of you who have never, *ever* juggled and have been too scared to even try....

It's not that scary really. Especially when you start with nylon scarves. I use them all the time and I juggle them outside when it's windy. But a handy tip is DON'T DO THIS, not to start with. Nylon scarves work well for juggling novices because they are so light that they move very slowly. However, the wind will blow them all over the place. I'm used to it, but if you're not, you'll spend all your practice time chasing after them. And then you'll get fed up, demoralized, and convinced that you'll *never* learn. And we don't want that!

So, get yourself a set of three nylon scarves, in different colors, find a place indoors out of wind, drafts (including fans, and air-conditioning or central heating vents), and we're ready to begin!

3

ONE AND TWO SCARVES

THE METHOD

Grasp one scarf in the center with your best hand. (This is the hand you write with usually, but it can be the other if you prefer!)

Toss it into the air so it crosses your chest, and catch it with your other hand. Simple, huh?

4

Toss it back. Do this ten times.

Now toss and clap your hands once before you catch it. Now try and clap twice.

CLAP

ACHOOO

Done that? We'll move on. Pick up the second scarf and hold one in each hand. This is the hard part. Get this right and the next page will be a piece of cake.

Imagine there is an X in front of you. Leading with your best hand, throw one scarf up one line of the X.

When this has reached its highest point and starts to fall, toss the second scarf up the other line of the X.

Say to yourself:

"Throw, throw, catch, catch."

5

THREE SCARVES

Managing okay? Make sure you throw both scarves and they change hands. No sneaky passing from hand to hand—that's playground juggling. Also, don't worry if you're not catching too well. Juggling is all about throwing. Get the timing right and the catching will come later!

Happy? Pick up the third scarf, then, and put it in your best hand. This hand should hold two scarves, one in the front and one in the back. Hold one scarf in the other hand.

Leading with the front scarf in the hand that holds two, throw just two scarves as you did in the previous exercise.

Now the moment has arrived to get the third scarf in. Throw scarf number One and when it reaches its peak and starts to fall, throw scarf number Two.

When Two reaches its peak and starts to fall, throw number Three. In the meantime you will have caught One, and so on. Hey! You're juggling, now! No problem, right?

If you can get up to 20 throws, you're performing the Three-Scarf Cascade! Which means you're ready for the trick on the next page.

7

HANDY TIP:
Keep your eye on the peaking scarf, not on your hands.

EYE SEE!

SIMPLE TRICK!

**So, here we are...
juggling! You've
conquered the Three-
Scarf Cascade, so now
try this simple trick:**

Put one hand, with scarf
attached, on your hip, then rotate
the two remaining scarves in a
clockwise direction.

Now revert back to your
Three-Scarf Cascade, then repeat

the one-arm rotation with the
other hand. Ta-da!—you have
your very first juggling routine!

FANCY START

How about this? Start with one scarf on your foot. Kick it up,
trying hard not to fall over, and then throw another scarf while
catching the kicked-up scarf. Watch out for the family dog or cat.
They won't appreciate a kick in the chops! Go into the
Three-Scarf Cascade.

ANOTHER SHAKY MOVE

While juggling, raise your best knee (that's the
one on the same side as your best hand).
Then, when your next best-hand throw
comes along, throw under the leg. Once
you get good at this, try throwing under
your not-so-best leg. Or toss behind
your back. This is a bit harder, but can
do wonders for your waistline! I refer
to all these moves as shaky because
it's fairly likely you'll fall over. So
practice these—for the first time—
somewhere soft and safe, away from
staircases, family pets, and expensive
china or keepsakes.

HARDER TRICKS

OK, let's try some of these harder moves with your scarves. This will give you some idea of the juggling method, which we will adapt later with beanbags.

THE COLUMN

Hold two scarves in one hand and the third in the other. Throw a scarf from each hand straight upward, then when they start to fall, throw the third scarf up the middle.

Catch the two falling scarves and throw again.

Then catch the third scarf and throw that.

Catch the two falling scarves and... Get it? You will if you try 'cause it's NOT THAT HARD. But just to complicate things, you can vary the paths of the scarves by throwing two up the middle and one up the side.

I CAN DO THAT!!

FEELING LONELY?

Then juggle with a partner. Find a friend who can juggle, but it's not necessary to be that good. In fact your friend doesn't need to be able to juggle at all. And you will only need one set of scarves.

Teach this:

Face your partner and stand a little ways apart. One of you holds two scarves in one hand and the other person holds the third. Put your other hand behind your back. You only need one hand for this.

I assume *you* will be holding the two scarves. Lead off with the first one and toss it to your friend.

When it's about halfway across, your friend should toss his/her scarf to you. In the meantime he/she will catch your scarf.

When your friend's scarf is about halfway across, guess what you do? Uh-huh. You toss your second scarf, and so on. You can also try this with basketballs if you want, but you will need to use both hands.

10

FRIENDLY JUGGLING

Okay. You enjoyed the juggling on the previous page so much that you and your friend are even greater friends. Here's some juggling for *friendly* people.

WARNING: It is inadvisable to try this with someone who doesn't like you!

Stand side by side. You can put your arm around your partner if you want. One of you holds two scarves and the other holds the other!

CAT-A-LOG

The one holding two starts and you both juggle as if you were joined down the middle, with two hands, two heads, and four legs.

We will be doing this move with beanbags later, with some extra embellishments.

11

JUGGLING FOUR

CRASH! You've fainted? Don't worry— juggling FOUR isn't *that* hard. In fact, since it's totally different from three, some people learn four FIRST. (Whether they can actually do it or not, I don't know, because I learned three first!)

The method for juggling four scarves is the same as four balls, so do this first and the other will come easier. (Get someone to revive you first, too. Hey! You can use one of the scarves!)

FIRST FOUR METHOD

You can start by doing it like this:

Hold two scarves in each hand.
Throw one from each hand up toward the center so that they follow a circle outward.

When they start to fall, throw the second pair of scarves and catch the first one. Throw them again, and again, and again....

MORE SCARVES, PALS

It's not that hard, is it? Oh, it is? What happened? You ended up with scarves draped all over your head? Hmm, yes, that does tend to happen. The only thing to do is to try again and again. Knot the scarves in the middle if you want. It might help. At least there will be less of the scarf to drape!

JUGGLING FOUR THE HARDER WAY

Yes, juggling four this way *is* pretty difficult. Not that I want to be a drag just as you are doing so well and everything, but this is the hardest thing that you have been asked to do so far!

Hold two scarves in each hand as you did before.

SO EASY!!

Now throw a scarf upward from your best hand and, immediately afterward, throw the first scarf from your other hand.

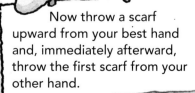

When they start to fall, throw your second scarves and catch the first ones. The best-hand throws should always be slightly ahead of the other hand. The throws are staggered, in other words. And be careful that they don't cross. You'll just lapse into the Three-Scarf Cascade if they do.

How did it go? You don't want to talk about it? I understand. Okay. Take comfort in the fact that you CAN do three. You CAN, can't you?

A FOUR-SCARF TRICK

This is way cool and (bonus) not that hard. It's Columns, but with four. You will be tossing with both hands, so you will have to devise your own best starting method. You can hold all four scarves together, or you can throw the front one in each hand first. (I find that that works for me.)

Lean one way and toss two scarves into the air together, then lean the other way and toss the other two.

Lean back, catch, then re-toss the first two. Now lean the other way, catch, then re-toss the second two. Phew! Did I say it was easy? It's really tiring. In fact, all work with scarves is tiring, since they require so much effort to throw in the first place.

Now, try this one. Two one side, two the other, lean back, catch... whoops, you've missed them. Ah well, this is also called Splits, so you've probably found out that you have to be pretty stretchy. Try to avoid actually doing a split, though. (For this reason, avoid doing this trick on a polished floor!)

SIX-SCARF JUGGLING

Finally, before we leave the scarf section of the Juggling Zone, we'll toss up six scarves (with a partner, of course). For this you will have to find a friend who can a) juggle a little and b) owns a set of three scarves. Tall order, eh? When you've tracked down such an ideal partner, try this:

Face each other about three feet (1 m) apart. You hold four scarves, two in each hand, and your partner holds the other two, one in each hand. You start by throwing the front two scarves to your partner. When they are about halfway across, your partner tosses his/her two scarves to you.

16

KEEP THOSE SCARVES COMING, PALS

SCARVES FOR SALE

HE ONLY WANTS ME FOR MY SCARVES

BEANBAGS

Hi! Welcome to the beanbag section of the Juggling Zone. Normally, I would say something like, "You will first need three beanbags, which you can pick up at any juggling store." But, as you will have already discovered (I hope), there are three beanbags attached to this book!

An additional "welcome" to those readers who skipped the scarf-juggling section altogether. Okay, so scarves weren't for you. Too bad! I'll be referring back to it continually, so go back to page 4 and read up!

Anyway... to begin. Beanbags are heavier than scarves and can do far more damage in the house, so pick a place to juggle that's away from the TV, sound system, light fixtures, etc.

Give your wrists a shake to get really loose, then take one beanbag in your best hand and put the other two bags down on the floor.

SHAKE

SHAKE

HEAVY MAN!

Now toss the beanbag into your other hand, following an arc just above your head. Keep your eyes on the peaking point of the beanbag.

Do this several times, just to get the feel of the beanbag and the way that it moves.

TWO AND THREE BEANBAGS

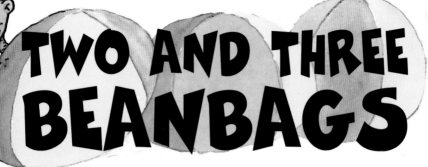

For those who STILL haven't bothered to read the scarf section, your best hand is the one you usually do most things with, like writing and scissor-cutting. However, you may use your other hand if you prefer.

Remember what we did with two scarves? We do the same thing with two beanbags. The difference is that beanbags move much faster, so there is less time to think.

Imagine there is an X in front of you. Toss one beanbag up one line of the X.

When it reaches its highest point and starts to fall, toss the second one up the other line. Say to yourself,

"throw, throw, catch, catch."

WHICH IS YOUR BEST HAND?

If you find this difficult (i.e. your brain thinks "ah, an-easy-way-of-getting-a-beanbag-from-one-hand-to-another-is-to-pass-it"), then don't try to catch, just throw. As soon as you have mastered the right rhythm, try to catch one beanbag, then the other. Your brain is trying to unscramble new messages and might be a little slow to start!

THREE BEANBAGS

I heard someone say on TV that you use the left side of your brain to master juggling. Then, once you have mastered it, it becomes a right-side-of-the-brain activity. Does this mean that to juggle, you only need half a brain? Hmm...

It's time to do the Three-Ball Cascade with beanbags. Put two beanbags in your best hand. Grip the back one with your ring and little finger. Hold the front one with the remaining fingers and thumb. Put the third beanbag in your other hand.

I THINK THAT'S HIS BEST HAND

Now, toss the first beanbag in the hand that holds two. When this has reached its highest point and starts to fall, toss the beanbag from the other hand. When *this* has reached its highest point and starts to fall, toss the third, then the fourth, fifth, sixth, and so on. (They're beanbags one, two and three the second time around!)

If you have read the scarf section, this will all be crystal clear (page 4 if you want to brush up).

VARYING THE THREE-BALL CASCADE

The secret of juggling can be summed up in one word... PRACTICE! If you find that you can't get past three throws initially, just keep at it. Suddenly, you will throw the fourth beanbag, then the fifth. Progress can be slow, but don't get discouraged. It took me six months! Once you *have* managed to do at least 20 throws though, you can try some of these easy variations:

• Vary your height and width, ceiling and fixtures permitting. Juggle high then low, narrow then wide.

• Play music and get with the beat! Talk to someone while you are juggling or look at something other than the beanbags.

• If constant dropping is getting on your nerves, juggle over a bed. At least you won't have to bend down very far. And if the throws tend to keep moving forward, try juggling against a wall.

• ALSO, TRY LYING ON THE FLOOR AND JUGGLING UPWARD. BUT DON'T DO THIS AFTER A HEAVY MEAL. A BEANBAG IN THE STOMACH CAN BE PRETTY UNCOMFORTABLE.

SOMETHING DIFFERENT

Here we are, then, juggling quite happily. Time to push ourselves a bit further. We're going to do Two-Ball. Yeah, yeah—so we've spent a lot of time fiddling around with three.... Why a whole page on two? The answer, it's two with one hand.

Put two beanbags in your best hand. Toss one up, and, when it peaks, toss the second one.

Catch the first one and toss again. You can either do this move in Columns, up and down, or the balls can go around in a circle. But always keep them in front of you. Start with high throws to give yourself time. Then gradually lower the toss until you feel that you have total control of the height.

WEAK HAND!

Once you have mastered this, do the hard part and try it with your weaker hand. Not so easy, huh? Work on this move—it will reap its rewards later. Actually, right in the next few pages.

CLAWING.

Before we move even farther into the Zone and start doing the tough stuff, I thought I'd include Clawing in our basics section.

By now (that is, IF you've waded through the scarf section), you will have noticed that the throw for scarves is different than the throw for beanbags. With the scarves, the juggled object is held with your palms facedown, whereas with the beanbags, it's faceup.

Just out of interest, let's juggle the beanbags with palms facedown. This is called Clawing, and it's a real hoot! Try with just one first.

You will have to toss backhanded and bring your other hand downward onto the falling beanbag.

Then give another backhanded toss.

Good, huh? Now try with two beanbags and then three. I told you it was a hoot!

JUGGLING ZONE
TOUGH STUFF

We've been through the basics now, and it's time to try hot, cool, and just plain tough stuff! This is no place for wimps, and to prove it to you, here's a trick called The Shower. Don't worry, you won't get wet!

Some of you may have struggled with this before you learned the Three-Ball Cascade. The Shower is when three beanbags are thrown around in a circle. One hand does all the throwing while the other does the catching. You have to throw really fast, so be careful where you practice this move!

| Start by holding two beanbags in your best hand. | Throw the first in a high arc to your other hand. |

Throw the second quickly behind it, so it's on its way before the first one lands. Do this ten times.

HAVE ANOTHER BALL

Then place the third beanbag into your other hand. Throw the two from your best hand, as detailed above, and just before the first one lands, pass the third beanbag into your best hand and throw it.

FASTER FASTER!

Keep passing and throwing, and the beanbags will fly around in circles. This fast-paced trick is likely to make you sweat, so you may get wet after all!

25

GO MAN GO!

THE REVERSE CASCADE

As the name suggests, this is opposite of the move we have already learned. So, *forget* all I told you about the Three-Ball Cascade and try this instead. Well, don't actually forget it, just put it to the side.

You recall that I suggested you imagine an X in front of you when you juggled the Three-Ball Cascade? Forget that and imagine, instead, that there is an upside-down U (or a horseshoe, if you're into that kind of thing).

Start by throwing a beanbag along the upside-down U path, above your head, into your other hand.

Release the beanbag at shoulder level and catch it at about waist level.
Repeat ten times or as many times as you like!

26

As soon as you are happy with this throw, introduce the second beanbag. Throw the first bag from your best hand.

When it reaches its highest point and starts to fall, throw the other bag over the TOP of it.

Get into a smooth rhythm, then work the third beanbag in. Remember, as soon as a beanbag peaks, throw the next one over the top of it.

OOPS.

You may get some midair collisions, but don't despair, it still happens to all of us.... OK, some of us. OK, it happens to me all the time!

27

MIX AND MINGLE

"Mix and Mingle" is a term I use for strolling street entertainment, but it fits here for mixing the Three-Ball and Reverse Cascades.

Start by doing a Three-Ball Cascade, then, on every sixth throw, whizz one around the upside-down U path.

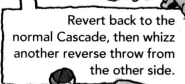

SHOW OFF.

Revert back to the normal Cascade, then whizz another reverse throw from the other side.

GOOD, HUH?

Go into the Reverse Cascade, then out again into the three ball. Mix it up. It's easy and looks really impressive.

Now mingle a bit. Start with the normal Cascade, then throw two reverse tosses, almost as if you are going into the Shower, but toss the third beanbag normally. (Does that make sense?) Go back to the normal Cascade, then repeat the two quick reverse tosses and the third normal one.

Keep up this marvelous feat for as long as you or your audience can take!

29

THE YO-YO
(or OY-OY)

What's a Yo-yo? It's a thing on a string, isn't it? So what's that got to do with juggling? Um, I dunno. I'm not even sure what this move is called, but it does end up *behaving* like a yo-yo!

Do you remember the page totally devoted to Two-Ball? You were thinking that that was a total waste of time, but here you will find your efforts rewarded. This move looks very impressive and isn't that hard, provided your left and right hands can work independently of each other.

NOT THAT YO-YO

Start by doing the Two-Ball in your best hand. Try to do them in columns, each with its own path.

Now raise your other hand so that you can see it alongside your Two-Ball move. Wave this hand about. Ha! Bet you dropped the beanbags! Pick them up and try again. This time, watch the path of one of the beanbags and follow it with your other hand.

WHAT, NO PADDLE?

WARNING:
Your best-hand movements should be twice as fast as your other hand. If they aren't, you're up the creek!

YO-YO

PART 2

Okay, let's assume that you can get one hand moving at half the speed of the other.

Now try holding a beanbag in this hand. Move it up and down, following the path of one of the other beanbags in your best hand. They'll look as though they're joined.

Now be *really* cool and move the beanbag in your weaker hand *above* the ball you are following. Move it up and down in time with it. It will look as if it is on an invisible string.

Practice these moves, because when perfected, they're really funny. The only drawback is that when you've suffered weeks practicing them, people (especially kids) will say that you're cheating and that it's not real juggling! So swing into the Three-Ball Cascade to keep them happy. (Such is life.)

SEESAW

This is really hard. I don't want to discourage you, but forewarned is forearmed. No amount of skimming though the scarf section will help with this little treat! It's known as "The Seesaw," and you'll go through lots of up and downs learning it! I'll get on with it right away.

To begin, place two beanbags in your best hand, one in the front and one in the back.

Place the third beanbag in your weaker hand. So far so good, huh? Feeling confident? Well, get a load of this....

WHAT... REALLY HARD?

Toss the front beanbag in the hand that holds two upward.

When it peaks and starts to fall, toss the beanbag from your weaker hand upward.

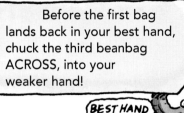

Before the first bag lands back in your best hand, chuck the third beanbag ACROSS, into your weaker hand!

BEST HAND

Before the second bag lands, toss the first ball up again and chuck the third ball back!

CRASH

Get it? Phew! It's made me sweat just writing it down. Don't worry if you don't get it right away, but be careful how you do the throw across. We don't want any broken windows!

HELPFUL HINT IF YOU ARE HAVING TROUBLE:

A useful tip is to replace beanbags One and Two with scarves. That way, you get the benefit of the slow-moving objects upward and the fast-moving object across. It's those scarves to the rescue again!

SCARVES AGAIN, PALS!!

COLUMNS

After the Seesaw, I think we need something a little easier. A skim through the scarf section will help with this next Columns maneuver. Of course, doing it with beanbags will have to be a little harder—that little extra move to make life more challenging!

Start with two beanbags in your best hand, and, you've guessed it, the other beanbag in your other hand!

Toss a beanbag from each hand directly upward into the air.

When they reach their highest point and start to fall, toss the third beanbag up the middle. Catch the first two and repeat.

Get into a smooth rhythm, up and down, up and down. Like a seesaw, isn't it?

For an extra challenge, toss the two bags so that they cross over in an arc and change hands. Toss the third up the center as usual. Keep one hand slightly back from the other so the bags don't collide, but if they do, try to catch them and act like you meant it. You can always instigate a midair collision as a variation, provided of course that you get the bags to fall back into your hands!

TRAPPING!

By now you've probably tried quite a few tricks. While you're taking a quick time-out, practice a few of these Trapping moves to work into your routine:

- Try stopping mid-juggle by catching a beanbag on the top of your hand. Trap it between the middle and ring fingers. Hold it for a while, then flip back into the Three-Ball Cascade. Practice catching and halting the beanbag on its own, for starters.

- Another trapping point is the shoulder. Toss the beanbag onto your shoulder and trap it with your neck. Be careful if you wear glasses or contact lenses. Break or lose them and you won't be juggling for quite some time.

- You can also trap with your foot and then flip it back into the routine.

As in all the other cases, practice Trapping with only one beanbag. Once you've mastered it, work the other two in.

GETTING PHYSICAL

We threw a scarf under the leg, so why not a beanbag? It's really simple—raise your best leg, bend your best knee, and the next time your best hand throws a beanbag, pass it under your leg. It didn't work, huh? What happened? You fell over? It hit your calf? You knocked out the cat?

Well, let's give you some tips. First, wear loose-fitting pants or stretchy leggings. You don't want clothes restricting your movement.

Now, when you lift your leg, turn it a little bit outward. This helps get your calf out of the way!

Okay, try again!

Start your Cascade by throwing under the leg. Then, when you are ready, raise your best leg and toss your next best-hand throw under it. Did it work that time? It will. You could help, too, by tossing your preceding throw a little bit higher to give yourself more time. Once again take care where you practice this.

GETTING PHYSICAL II

A lot of these moves can be done with different objects. The following, I suggest, is best done with beanbags or other light balls.

We are going to use parts of the body to bounce our beanbags. You can bounce beanbags off the wrist, elbow, forehead, knee, toe, or even forearm. Once again, the secret is to first practice with just one beanbag. Soccer-playing jugglers should find this easy, but others will have to work at it a bit. Check that cats and other pets are well out the way. You know what dogs are like—they have to sniff everything!

Once you've mastered the move, bounce into the Cascade, start juggling, and then bounce a beanbag off a part of your body as part of your routine. Don't try to bounce one off the floor. Beanbags don't bounce, and we will be doing Floor Juggling later on.

39

TIME FOR A SNACK

No, this isn't a coffee break. I thought we could try juggling and eating something at the same time. An apple springs to mind. You can do this two ways, one easy and one hard.

Easy one first: Take three pieces of fruit and vegetable, like an apple, a potato, and an orange. Decide which one you want to eat. I recommend the apple.

Juggle all three in a Cascade, then suddenly transfer the potato and the orange to one hand and take a bite from the apple. Resume juggling. Juice will spray everywhere and the audience—if you have one—will either:

1. Be impressed.

or

2. Call you a cheater.

CHEATER !!

Juggle again, maintain the potato and orange in Two- Ball mode, and then take another bite. If they still call you a cheater, stop and finish your apple in peace. Wipe your hands because this can be messy.

JUGGLING AND EATING THE PROPER WAY!

First, clean up a beanbag and use it as a substitute apple.

Start to juggle. When the clean beanbag comes into your best hand, toss the next throw high and bring the clean beanbag up to your mouth.

Resume juggling normally.

When you feel up to it, try bringing the clean beanbag up to your mouth again.
Do this every sixth time the bag comes into your best hand, then every third time, eventually doing it every time.

NOW CLEAN THAT UP!

Now you can use an apple and really get going. Be daring and use a potato, an egg, or even a chocolate bar. Eggs are fun, but you can cheat and hard-boil them first (although, if you drop a hard-boiled egg, it still makes a mess).

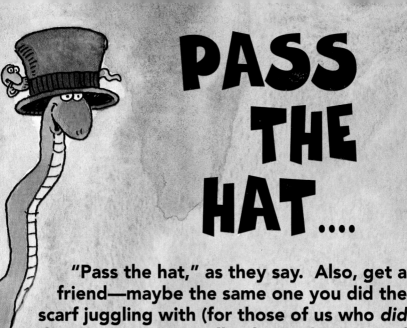

PASS THE HAT....

"Pass the hat," as they say. Also, get a friend—maybe the same one you did the scarf juggling with (for those of us who *did* that section). You will only need one set of beanbags, so yours will do!

Remember the Friendly Juggling, when you acted as though you were joined at the hip? When two people juggled three scarves as if they were one person? Well, you can do this with beanbags, too. And just to make it more fun, get a hold of an old hat, a silly cap, or other headgear.

Stand side by side with three beanbags. If you stand on the right, use your right hand only. The other person uses his or her left. In your left hand hold the hat.

You hold the two beanbags and start to juggle. When you have the Cascade going nicely, pass the hat onto your partner's head. Your partner, in turn, passes it back to your head, and so on.

Get other props if you want, like fake glasses or a clown nose, and pass them from head to head.

DON'T SAY ANYTHING!

As a neat ending to this juggle, pull another beanbag out of your pocket, and at an agreed moment, step forward and juggle alone, leaving your partner with the getup on and the extra beanbag!

STEALING TIME

While you're still
friendly with your partner
and you still only have
three beanbags,
try this:

THIS IS THE EASY PART

Let your partner juggle three while you stand and watch.
Then, when you are ready, take the beanbags from your
partner and juggle the beanbags yourself.

GOING AROUND IN CIRCLES

A more skillful version of the previous trick is when your partner actually tosses the beanbags to you.

Start side by side; and on the given word, have your partner toss the bags to you. If you are standing on your partner's left, the pass will be a right-handed throw. If you are on your partner's right, it will be a left-handed throw. To make life easier, if you are right-handed, find a left-handed juggler. But that's not absolutely necessary.

OKAY... THROW

WHEEE

Get it? Okay, now try it several times, with you or your partner running around to the other side to catch the beanbags.

Now try this standing behind your partner. Instead of throwing sideways, throw backward and then run around the back for your turn. The backward throw is pretty tricky, so practice with just one beanbag first.

FIVE BEANBAGS

(and a partner!)

To do this you will have to find a partner who has some juggling balls, or maybe you can borrow another set. But if your partner is the same one who has been with you all through this book, then isn't it time that they got some gear of their own?

Stand side by side. You hold three beanbags and your partner holds two.

Start juggling, and on a given number, throw one beanbag to your partner.

I CAN'T BEAR TO LOOK

Your partner then juggles, and on a given number, tosses the bag back to you.

Repeat as often as you like, and even try passing something different, like an egg or a potato.

If you have friends who can juggle, play this game in a circle: Your friends each hold two and you—it's your idea—hold three.

Start juggling and then toss to a person of your choice (without telling that person, of course!).

CATCH IT!!

BUT I CAN'T CATCH IT

That person must catch, juggle, and then toss to another person. Whoever drops it is out. You could make the game more friendly by calling the person's name first.

SIDEWAYS WITH 6.

Let's assume your partner read the last page and was shamed into buying his or her own set of beanbags. If not, you won't be able to do any of the following three pages!

Stand side by side again, both juggling three beanbags. Try to juggle at the same speed.

Then, on a given number, you pass one ball to each other. One tosses high over the juggling pattern, the other goes low, just so you don't get any midair collisions! You can decide who's going to do what yourselves. (If you've gotten this far, you don't need that kind of advice from me, anyway.)

You can also choose how far away from each other you want to stand. Some people prefer six feet, others just three. It's NO BIG DEAL!

HE CAN'T BE SERIOUS.

SUE!

BOB!

TOM, GRAB THE STRIPED BALL

· If your friends are still talking to you after page 49's passing game, try this one with them. But you'll have to shout out names, because they have to toss a beanbag back to you! Get as many people as you can tossing beanbags simultaneously, and create chaos!

51

PASSING

A word of warning: This can cause arguments. Agree beforehand with your partner not to start a fight, make false accusations, or call each other names.... Remember, *no one* is perfect.

You will need a partner who is as good—or as bad—as you are. You will also need a set of beanbags each.

There are lots of different patterns for Passing, but I'll tell you about the two that work best for me. (Although, they *did* nearly cause a divorce once.)

Stand facing each other about six feet (2 m) apart. Put two beanbags in your right hand and one in the left. If you're a left-handed juggler, you'll just have to bow to handism and juggle right-handed!

Raise your hands to shoulder height and then one of you has to say "go," or you won't start.

On the command, lower your hands and start juggling at the same speed and the same height. It might help if one of you calls out the throws so you keep together.

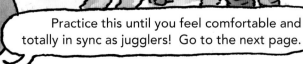

Practice this until you feel comfortable and totally in sync as jugglers! Go to the next page.

PASSING II

Happy? We'll move on.

What happens next is that on every third throw you toss the ball to your partner. So your throw goes from your right hand into his or her left hand, and vice versa. If this is too frequent, try the pass on every sixth throw. The beanbag is then absorbed into your Cascade.

CONFUSING, ISN'T IT?

CRUNCH

Does this make sense? Try it and see. Well, how did it go? Are both of you still speaking?

Some common faults are that passes are not accurate, too high, off course, and, in some cases, following throws can fly forward, too. In fact, you can get yourself into a big mess, but I warned you about that! Just keep trying. Juggle together, and then on every third or sixth throw, pass the beanbag from your right hand to your partner's left. What could be easier?

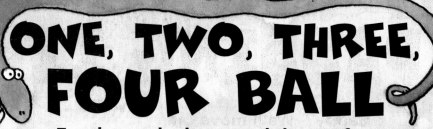

ONE, TWO, THREE, FOUR BALL

For those who have read the scarf section, congratulations. You'll know just what to do here. Four-Ball juggling is two in each hand, just like the scarves. Except that now, of course, we're using beanbags. There's less time to think and reactions have to be quicker.

> So, to recap: Hold two beanbags in each hand. Toss one from each hand into the air in a circle outward.

> When it peaks and starts to fall, throw the second one in a circle outward.

Now repeat this, except make the circle inward. Not too hard, huh? Do *not* let the beanbags cross. Juggled objects do not cross in Four-Ball.

Here's the big test. Can you do the staggered throws? Give yourself plenty of room. If you are indoors and the ceiling is low, kneel down. If that's uncomfortable, then go outside. If the weather is bad, well, then you'll just have to wait and try again later.

THE STAGGERED FOUR-BALL

STAGGER

And you *will be* once you start doing this. Or your friends will be!

Four-Ball juggling looks very impressive, but it has to move very quickly. Throw the first beanbag from your best hand straight upward.

Follow this immediately with an upward toss with the first beanbag in your weaker hand.

When they peak and start to fall, toss your second beanbags. The throws from your weaker hand should always be slightly behind your best hand.

A QUICK TRICK

Hold two beanbags in each hand.
Toss one from each hand together, so that they cross over at a point above head height.

Toss the one from your best hand higher so that it passes over the other beanbag.

When they start to fall, toss the other two in the same way. The beanbags will cross over and change hands, which contradicts what I said on page 54, but this trick is designed to bewilder you!

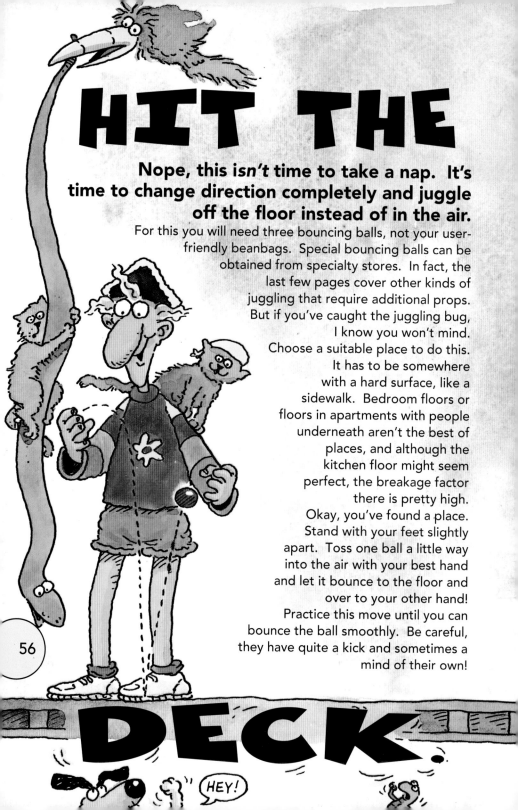

HIT THE

Nope, this isn't time to take a nap. It's time to change direction completely and juggle off the floor instead of in the air.

For this you will need three bouncing balls, not your user-friendly beanbags. Special bouncing balls can be obtained from specialty stores. In fact, the last few pages cover other kinds of juggling that require additional props. But if you've caught the juggling bug, I know you won't mind. Choose a suitable place to do this. It has to be somewhere with a hard surface, like a sidewalk. Bedroom floors or floors in apartments with people underneath aren't the best of places, and although the kitchen floor might seem perfect, the breakage factor there is pretty high. Okay, you've found a place. Stand with your feet slightly apart. Toss one ball a little way into the air with your best hand and let it bounce to the floor and over to your other hand! Practice this move until you can bounce the ball smoothly. Be careful, they have quite a kick and sometimes a mind of their own!

56

DECK

HEY!

FLOOR JUGGLING...
THE CASCADE

Once you are happy with the first move, go on to the second ball. Hold a ball in each hand.

Toss ball number One from your best hand and let it bounce.

Just before catching it, toss ball number Two and catch ball number One . Ball number Two will bounce right into your empty best hand!

Introduce the third ball like this: Hold two in your best hand and the other in the other! Lead off with the front one in your best hand and *just do it*. The secret is that just before you catch, you toss the next ball. Once you have this at your fingertips, try juggling in the air and then letting every sixth throw drop and bounce back. You can also try this with scarves. (Yeah, right.)

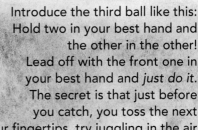

THE BUG

Have you caught it—the juggling bug, that is? If so, these final pages will tell you how to juggle other, much harder objects, which you will have to buy. They are more expensive than bouncing balls and only available at specialty stores. Yes, I'm talking about rings and clubs.

RINGS

Get a set of rings that suits you. It's better to go to a store and try them out before buying them. Juggling rings is the same as juggling beanbags, except that they are lighter, bigger, and can be thrown a lot higher. In fact, the higher they go, the better, so again: *don't juggle with them at home!*

Find somewhere with a high ceiling, like a gym, or try outside. Unfortunately, rings are easily blown around by the wind and they can hurt your fingers. Not that I'm trying to change your mind. Ring juggling is really a lot of fun. So start with just one and toss from your best hand to the other. You can hold your hands up and reach up and catch rings. The rings' path is narrower than beanbags', probably because they're so skinny.

TWO AND THREE RINGS

Now try the two throws—one ring in each hand, leading off with your best hand. Give the ring a spin as you throw to help make it more stable. Like a kite, they can be skittish.

Throw the first ring, and when it reaches its highest point and starts to fall, throw the second ring. Sounds familiar, huh? Be careful how you catch. Rings are made from a hard material, so if you catch them wrong, you'll scratch your fingers. If this is a problem, try juggling with gloves. But that might cause grip problems, so maybe you'll just have to stock up on bandages.

All right. Pick up the third ring and work it in.

Put two in your best hand. Grip the third ring with the ring and little fingers and the first ring with the other two and thumb. I don't need to tell you this. We've been through it loads of times. Just get on with it!

HANDY TIP:

Tilt your head upward and try to keep as narrow a path as you can. And go as high as you can without losing control.

CLUB LAND

Hi! Welcome to the Juggling Clubs Zone. If you haven't read any of this book so far, then forget it, unless you're a good juggler. You have to know the basics before you try this.

Clubs, like rings, have to be bought from juggling stores. The advice is the same. Go to the store and buy a set that fits you. There are many varieties, with different sizes, weights, and prices. Get some with soft handles, if you can, otherwise you'll be reaching for the first-aid kit again.

Another point to consider is that if you plan to juggle clubs with a partner at some stage, it helps to have similar-sized clubs. So keep that in mind, too. No jokes, now, this is serious.

Hold the club level in your best hand at a 45 degree angle to your body, so it isn't exactly in front of you. Put your thumb on the spot where the handle starts to widen.

OOPS WRONG CLUB

Sweep the club down to your side, then bring it back up again.

Release the club as it reaches the center of your body. It should make one flip in the air, then catch it by the handle in your other hand.

Remember, keep it at a 45 degree angle to the body. Repeat this one-club toss method until you can do it quite smoothly with both hands.

Now move onto two. Give yourself plenty of room and make the tosses pretty high to give yourself more time.

TWO CLUBS

Toss club number One and, as it starts to spin over, toss the number Two. The spin or flip equates with the peaking of a beanbag. In other words, after it's flipped, it's gonna fall!

BULLY!

Pause between each set of throws. Repeat this move and do not go onto three until you are ready. Go back to one if you have any problems. It might be boring, but it'll pay off in the end, when you master club control. (Sounds good?)

THREE OF CLUBS.

We're ready. We've practiced till we're sick of two clubs, and now we want to do three.

So put one club in each hand. Put the other club in the front of your best hand. The back club is held by the ring and little fingers, the front club is held by the thumb and remaining two. Heard that before? Well, there's a slight difference—your index finger should rest along the neck of the club.

As it flips over, toss number Two. Catch One.

As club number Two flips over, toss number Three. Catch Two and then catch Three.

WOW! DID I DO THAT?

63

And there you have it!

TIPS

Well, we've penetrated the Juggling Zone right into the Club Land. You can do as many tricks and things with a partner in Club Land as you can in Beanbag Land. You can also go on to doing lots of Ring Juggling, as long as you can get all the gear.

Practice every day if you can. Juggling is very relaxing if you are stressed out by work, school, or little sisters. If you find any particular move difficult, keep at it, or go back to the one before and try that one again. Don't be discouraged if someone else gets it quicker than you do! Everyone learns at their own pace. It really *did* take me six months, and now that I teach juggling, I see people learn in about six minutes. Get Grandma doing it—there's no upper age limit. And your dentist, too! Improving his or her dexterity will also benefit *you*!

Juggling's like riding a bike—once you've got it, you keep it. And it gives a whole new approach to grocery shopping. No more dropping cans of soup on your feet—your hand-eye coordination will be so sharp, you'll catch them before they hit the deck! Anyway, it's time I took off.

HAPPY JUGGLING, FOLKS!